Ojibwe Giizhig Anang Masinaa'igan

Ojibwe Sky Star Map Constellation Guidebook

An Introduction to Ojibwe Star Knowledge

Annette S. Lee
William Wilson
Jeff Tibbetts
Carl Gawboy

Ojibwe Giizhig Anang Masinaa'igan – Ojibwe Sky Star Map Constellation Guidebook

First published in June 2014
Layout and editing by A. M. Fellegy, Avenue F Productions, Cloquet MN 55720
Printed by Lightning Source-Ingram Spark, North Rocks, CA 99999

Cover art: *Ojibwe Giizhig Anang Masinaa'igan – Ojibwe Sky Star Map* by Annette S. Lee and William Wilson

ISBN 978-0-615-98678-4

http://web.stcloudstate.edu/planetarium/native_skywatchers.html

Ojibwe Giizhig Anang Masinaa'igan

OJIBWE GIIZHIG ANUNG MASINAAIGAN
Ojibwe Sky Star Map

ZIIGWAN ~ Spring

Mishi Bizhiw, Curly Tail, Great Panther

Madoodiswan, Sweat Lodge

Ikwe'anung, Women's Star, Venus

Waabun'anung, Morning Star

Ningobi'anung, Evening Star

NIIBIN ~ Summer

Ajiijaak/Bineshi Okanin, Crane/Skeleton Bird

Noondeshin Bemaadizid, Exhausted Bather

Nanaboujou, Nanaboujou

Giizis, Sun

Dibik-giizis, Night Sun, Moon

Ishpeming, Sky Above, Universe

BIBOON ~ Winter

Biboonkeonini, Wintermaker

Maingan Mikan, Wolf Trail, Ecliptic

Jiibaykona, Spirit Path, Milky Way

Jiibay Ziibi, River of Souls, Milky Way

Gwiingwa, Shooting star, Meteor

Anung Nibwakawin, Star Wisdom

DAGWAAGIN ~ Fall

Mooz, Moose

Bugonagiizhig, Hole in the Sky, Pleiades

Madoo'asinik, Sweating Stones, Pleiades

Waawaate, Aurora Borealis, Northern Lights

Jiibayag niimi'idiway, Spirits Dancing, Aurora Borealis

Gaagige Giizhig, Forever Sky, Universe

Maang, Loon   *Giwedin'anung*, North Star, Polaris   *Ojiig*, Fischer

GIWEDINANG ~ North

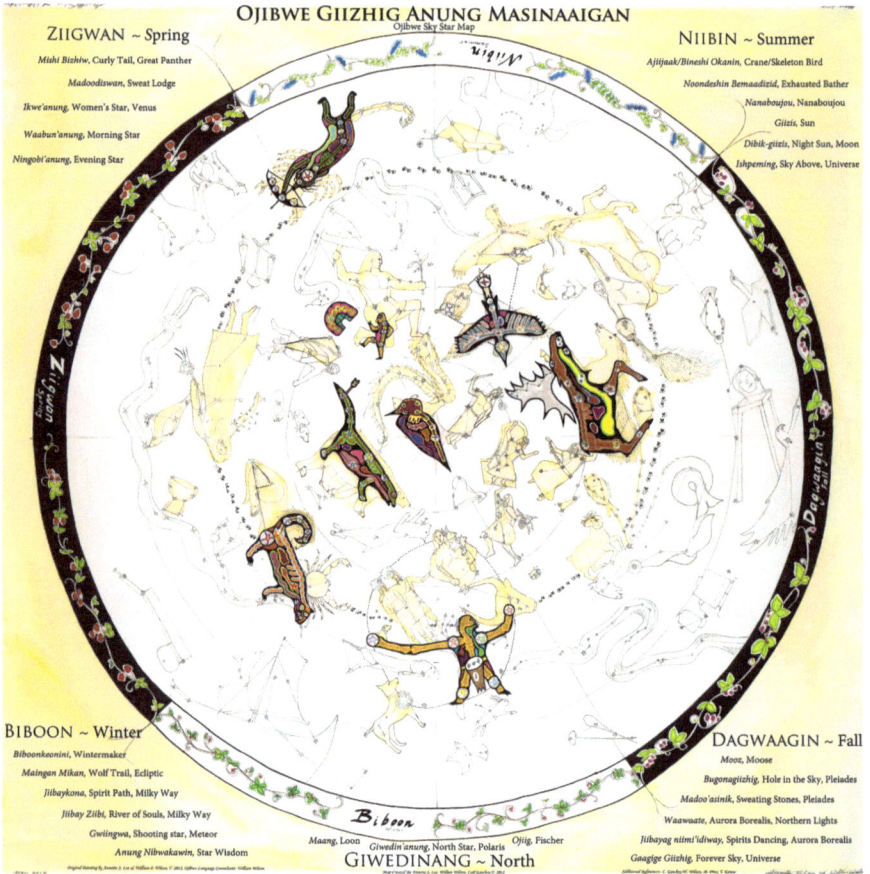

Fig. 1. Ojibwe Giizhig Anung Masinaa'igan

INTRODUCTION

Native Skywatchers

In the Ojibwe language, the Big Dipper is known as *Ojiig,* the Fisher [1] and in D(L)akota star knowledge, the same group of stars is seen as *To Win/TonWin* Blue Woman/Birth Woman [2]. In each, there are stories and teachings that help guide, teach, and inspire native peoples. This book is an outgrowth of Native Skywatchers research and programming, which focuses on understanding the Ojibwe and D(L)akota importance of these and other celestial connections. We seek to address the crisis of the loss of the indigenous star knowledge, specifically the Dakota and Ojibwe who are the native peoples of Minnesota. Our purpose is to remember, rebuild, and revitalize the native star knowledge.

There is urgency to this project for two reasons: 1) Native star knowledge is disappearing as elders pass. One Ojibwe elder spoke of his vision of "the star medicine returning through the native youth." He specifically called them "star readers" [3]. In 2011, he passed away suddenly. 2) The Minnesota State Science Standards for K-12 education require an "understanding that men and women throughout the history of all cultures, including Minnesota American Indian tribes and communities, have been involved in engineering design and scientific inquiry. . . .for example, Ojibwe and Dakota knowledge and use of patterns in the stars to predict and plan" [4]; yet, there is a complete lack of materials.

As with many North American tribes, much cultural knowledge, especially cultural astronomy, has been lost. The goal of the Native Skywatchers programming is to build community around native star knowledge. Native Skywatchers research and programming seeks out and brings together elders, culture teachers, language experts, and community members to discuss Ojibwe and D(L)akota star knowledge. Together, we have created two astronomically accurate and culturally important star maps, *Ojibwe Giizhig Anang Masinaa'igan* – Ojibwe Sky Star Map and *Makoçe Wiçanhpi Wowapi* – D(L)akota Sky Star Map, which were first disseminated to regional educators at a Native Skywatchers Middle School Teacher workshop in June 2012. In addition, we have developed hands-on curriculum that combines astronomy, culture, language, and art.

About the Ojibwe Sky Star Map

Ojibwe Giizhig Anang Masinaa'igan – Ojibwe Sky Star Map is a collaborative work between Annette Lee, William Wilson, and Carl Gawboy. The Ojibwe constellation identification is a result of the research and work of Carl Gawboy over a forty-year period [5].

The map is organized with Polaris, the North Star, in the center. This emphasizes the closeness of Polaris to our current North Celestial Pole and circumpolar motion. Because of circumpolar motion, we appear to see all the stars in the night sky revolve around the North Star in a counterclockwise motion as the hours pass each night into day. Because of this motion, in some native cultures the North Star is seen as one of the leaders of the star nation. Stars near the North Star do not set below the horizon. These are referred to as "North Circumpolar Stars." Note that the "northern stars" referred to in this book are the circumpolar stars as seen from approximately 45-55° N latitude, 85-110° W longitudes.

All stars not circumpolar, as seen from 45-55° N latitude, rise in the East and set in the West at regular times throughout the year. They are seasonal stars. The *Ojibwe Giizhig Anang Masinaa'igan* – Ojibwe Sky Star Map is arranged in order to show the constellations that are best visible each season. This assumes a viewing time of a few hours after sunset. In the night sky, stars of each season can be seen best overhead or in the South during that particular season. For example, if you look at the stars in the early summertime a few hours after sunset, you will see Hercules overhead and Scorpio low on the southern horizon. These are summer stars.

William Wilson used traditional Ojibwe x-ray style to paint the Ojibwe constellations. This style is symbolic of seeing the unseen. It is an allegory for the material world and the spirit world. The brightly colored internal organs and anatomical shapes are a glimpse into the inner layers of our bodies. Wilson explains, "We are seeing the picture as the spirits see us. They see right through. The strange looking animals and figures are portrayed as they come in ceremony. Sometimes they are half beaver, half eagle. Sometimes they are scary. Sometimes tempting." The border of the map includes strawberries, raspberries, blueberries, and winterberries (traditional Ojibwe foods) illustrated in reference to Ojibwe-style floral beadwork. Often, floral beadwork is done on black velvet or with a white beadwork background, usually on items of spiritual or social importance, such as pipe bags, moccasins, and leggings.

Lake Hegman Pictographs

Some of the Ojibwe constellations were painted long ago in pictographs on rocks in the Boundary Waters Canoe Area in northern Minnesota and Ontario, Canada [6]. For example, high up on the cliffs at North Lake Hegman, the *Mooz* constellation is painted on the rock face, complete with a heart line of stars. To the left of *Mooz* is the Ojibwe Wintermaker constellation and the *Gaadidnaway* – Curly Tail/*Mishibizhii* – Mountain Lion constellation. Carl

Fig. 2. North Hegman Lake Pictographs

Gawboy was the first person to understand that some of the rock paintings in the Boundary Waters Canoe Area are actually Ojibwe constellations [7].

Acknowledgements

The Ojibwe language varies from region to region and reservation to reservation. As a language still new to written form, Ojibwe spelling conventions are only in the beginning stages. In this text, the original titles of artwork have been retained; the body of the work follows the speakers of northern Minnesota and *A Concise Dictionary of Minnesota Ojibwe*.

The Native Skywatchers project acknowledges the elders and others who have kept this star knowledge alive. We acknowledge Paul Schultz (White Earth) who passed away suddenly in 2011 and Albert White Hat Sr. (Rosebud) who passed away in June 2013. Both men were collaborators with this project.

Funding to support this work has been provided by: NASA-Minnesota Space Grant, the Bush Foundation, Women's Foundation of Minnesota, NSF-North Star STEM Alliance, Minnesota State Arts Board, St. Cloud State University, and Fond du Lac Tribal and Community College. *Miigwech. Pidamaya/Pilamaya.* Thank you.

GIIWEDINONG ANANGOOG – NORTH CIRCUMPOLAR STARS

Ojiig – Fisher – Big Dipper/Ursa Major

The *Ojiig* constellation relates to the story of when the birds and spring were held prisoner by the ogres. Of all the animals, it was only the fisher that was able to trick the ogres and free the birds. He saved everyone with his courage and wit [8]. The fisher is one of the few animals that can kill and eat porcupines. It is not diurnal or nocturnal but, instead, prefers to eat

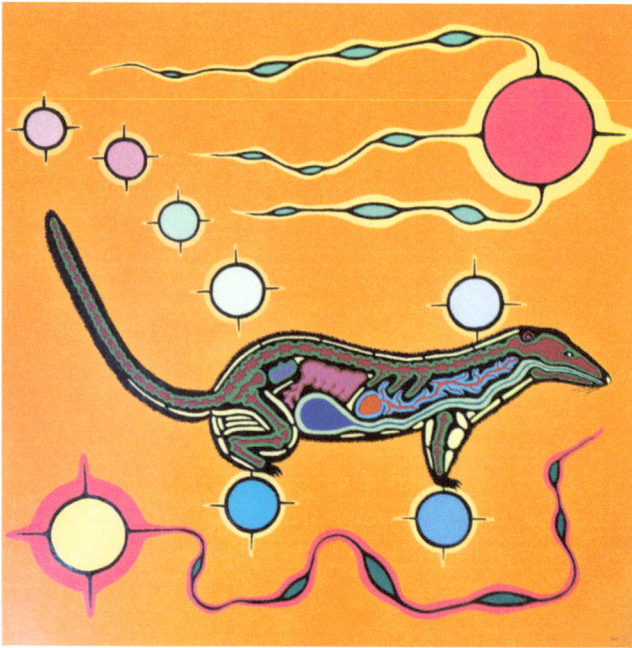

Fig. 3. Ojiig

and sleep as needed, often not at regular day/night intervals. Unlike most animals, the fisher tends not to build a home in one place and return to it but, rather, makes its den in different places. It is constantly on the move. *Ojiig* – Fisher constellation mirrors the behavior of the animal fisher. The *Ojiig* constellation is constantly moving around the North Celestial Pole day and night, year after year. The correlation between sky and earth, or above and below, is an important underlying cultural theme in Ojibwe star knowledge and reflects a keen sense of observation.

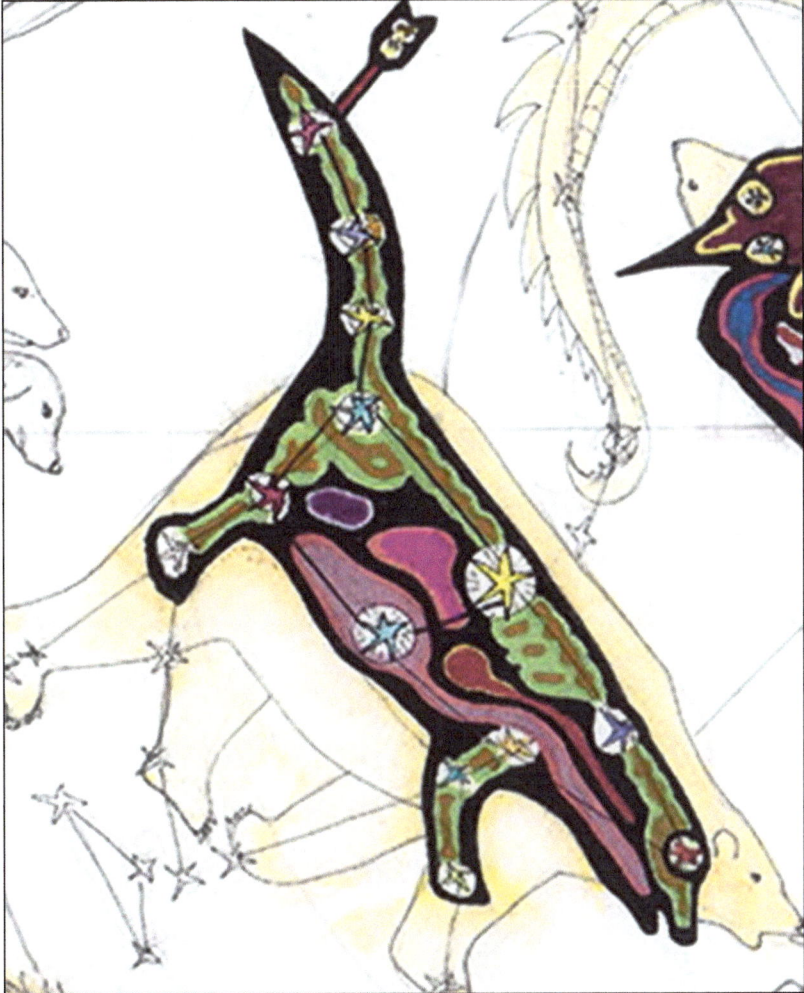

Fig. 4. Ojiig "Fisher"/Big Dipper "Ursa Major"

Fig. 5. Maang "Loon"/Little Dipper "Ursa Minor"

Maang – Loon – Little Dipper/Ursa Minor

The stars in the Little Dipper (Ursa Minor) make up the Ojibwe *Maang* – Loon constellation. The loon is one of the Ojibwe clans and is seen as an important messenger and leader [9]. The loon always stays close to the water, at the doorway between the sky above and the earth below. It sits on calm waters, then dives down to catch fish. Its survival depends on clear water. Loons' legs and feet are positioned very far back, and they cannot walk well on land; therefore, they avoid leaving the water. The word "loon" originates from the Old English word "lumme" meaning awkward or the Scandianavian word "lum" meaning lame or clumsy [10]. Preferring larger lakes, the loon only goes on land to nest.

The *Maang* – Loon constellation contains an important star in the night sky, the *Giiwedin Anang* or the North Star (Polaris). The pattern of white spots on a black background along the loon's back is reminiscent of a starry night sky. Traditionally, when the *maang* – loon was hunted for food, it was said to keep the body of the loon upright, the way it sleeps, out of respect.

Fig. 6. Ishpiming Maang (Loon in the Sky)

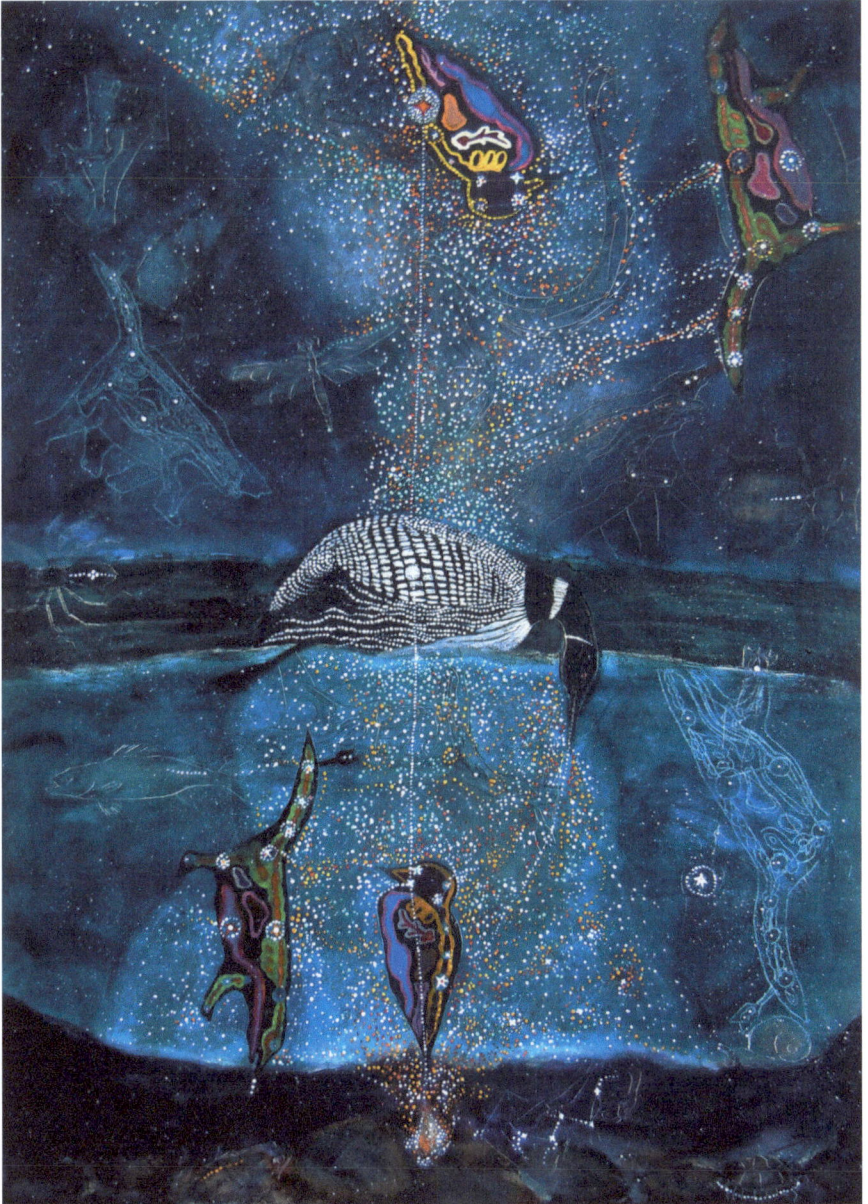

Fig. 7. Maang (Loon) - Doorkeeper of the North

Astronomical Treasures in the North Circumpolar Sky

Hubble Deep Fields

Over ten days in December 1995, the Hubble Space Telescope stared at a patch of dark sky the size of a grain of sand held at arm's length (2.5" across). In this speck of sky a 24-millionth of the entire sky, over 3,000 distinct galaxies were found. Many of these galaxies are the farthest and oldest objects ever seen by human eyes. These old galaxies appear smaller, more disturbed and irregular than those closer to us.

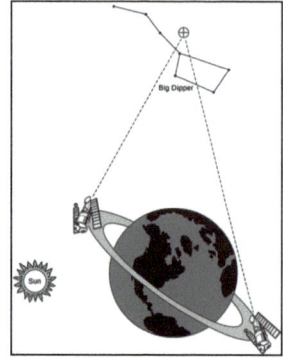

Fig. 8. Hubble Deep Field Observing Geometry

Fig. 9. Hubble Deep Field

When looking far away in astronomy, we are actually looking back in time because of the time it takes light to travel across vast distances. We are looking back to nearly the beginning of the Universe (13.8 billion years ago) at galaxies roughly twelve billion years old. In 2004 and 2012, similar images were made with the Hubble Ultra-Deep Field and the Hubble Extreme Deep Field. Taking pictures within the constellation Fornax (below Orion) at exposure times of one-million and then two-million seconds (eleven days and twenty-two days), the Hubble cameras found 10,000 and 5,000 galaxies.

Delta Cephei

In one corner of the Greek constellation Cepheus the King, we see Delta Cephei, a star that appears noticeably dimmer over roughly a five-day period. As this dying star desperately tries to find balance, the outer layers are pulsing and expanding like a beating heart. The time it takes for the pattern to repeat, or period, can be correlated to how bright the star really is: the longer the period, the brighter the star. Using this information, we can find the distance to the star. Delta Cephei is called a "standard candle" and is useful to find distances. In the 1920s, Edwin Hubble found a Cepheid variable star in the Andromeda "Nebula" and was able to calculate its distance. This showed everyone that the Andromeda "Nebula" was actually outside of our Milky Way Galaxy, and it has ever since been called the Andromeda Galaxy.

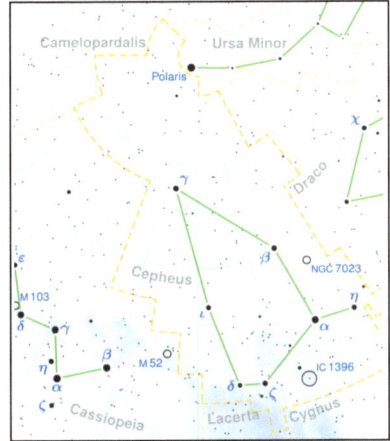

Fig. 10. Cepheus Constellation Map

Polaris, Thuban, and Precession

In Ojibwe, *Giiwedin Anang* is Polaris or the North Star. It is the only star in our sky that appears motionless, which is due to its current location less than 1° from the North Celestial Pole or Earth's northern rotational axis projected into space. An interesting point to keep in mind: due to the gravitational pull of the Sun and Moon on Earth, our rotational axis wobbles slightly. This can only be seen over thousands of years. Always about a 23.5° tilt from vertical, the axial tilt wobbles or processes in a circle in an approximately 26,000 year period. Consequently, Polaris will not always be the North Star. For example, 5,000 years ago (3,000 BC), Thuban was "the motionless star" or the North Star for the ancient Egyptians. Twelve thousand years from now, the bright star Vega will be somewhat close to the North Celestial Pole. Of all the North Stars, Polaris is the brightest and closest to the North Celestial Pole. We are living in "The Age of Polaris."

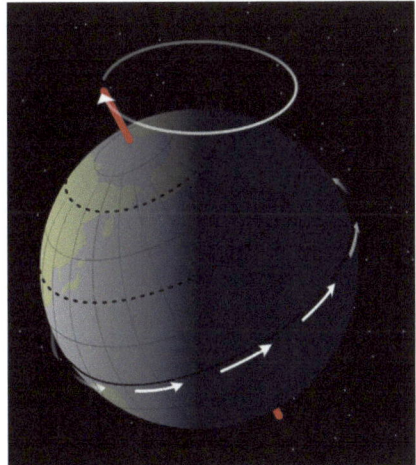

Fig. 11. Earth Precession

ZIIGWAN ANANGOOG – SPRING STARS

Gaadidnaway – Curly Tail/*Mishibizhii* – Great Panther – Leo and Hydra

Fig. 12. North Lake Hegman Pictographs

Gaadidnaway is a mountain lion/cougar/puma that was once more abundant in Minnesota than it is today. The big spirit cat lives at the bottom of lakes like *Gichigami* (Lake Superior) and can cause flooding or water danger. Curly Tail rises in late winter and is overhead in spring. The Ojibwe people knew that when the great cat was overhead the ice would be thawing, and it would be dangerous to cross lakes or rivers. Traditionally, this signaled the time to move from winter camp to sugar bush camp. At sugar bush, feasts and prayers are offered for the water spirits, such as *Gaadidnaway* – Curly Tail, and to all those relatives that did not survive the winter. *Gaadidnaway* – Curly Tail/*Mishibizhii* – Great Panther constellation is associated with the water. Note: The Greek constellation, Leo, a lion, overlaps with the "Ojibwe lion." In addition, the head of Curly Tail is located in the Greek constellation Hydra, the water snake.

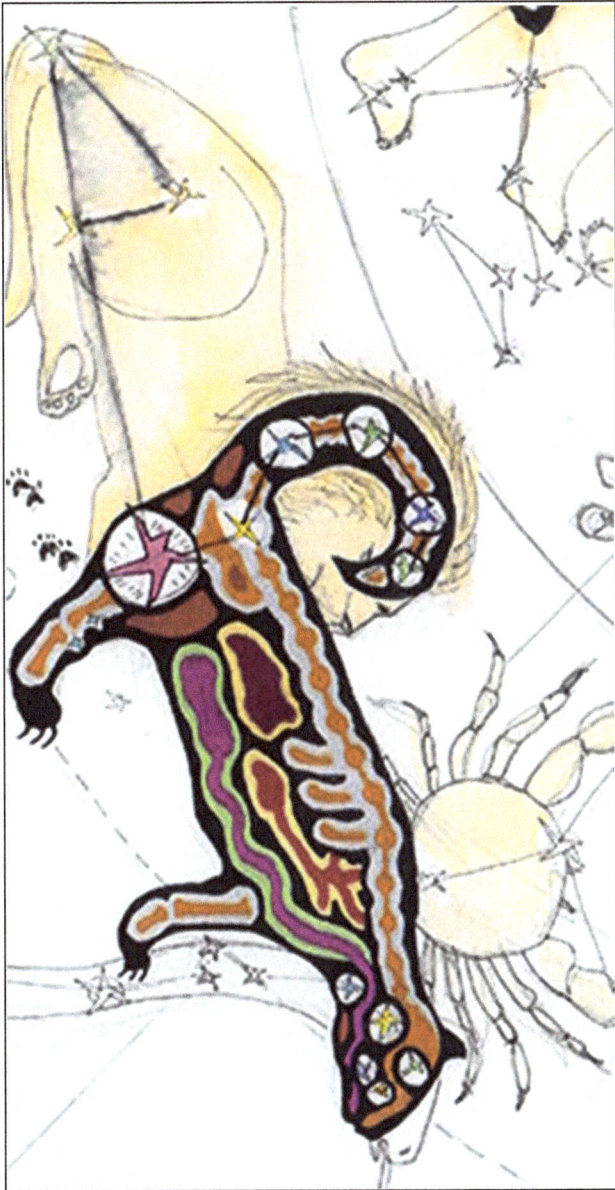

Fig. 13. Gaadidnaway – Curly Tail

Fig. 14. Madoodiswan (Sweat Lodge)

Fig. 15. Iskigamizigan (Sugar Bush Camp)

Fig. 16. Nookomiss Kikino'amagewin (Grandmother Teaching)

Madoodiswan –
Sweat Lodge – Corona

The sweat lodge is a purification
ceremony. It is about returning to the
womb and remembering/renewing a
person's spirit. The teaching is that
human beings are made of body, mind,
heart, and spirit. The spirit leads. The
Sweat Lodge is seen overhead in late
spring.

Fig. 17. Zaabibagaa and Spring Stars

Astronomical Treasures in the *Ziigwan Giizhig* – Spring Sky

Fig. 18. Virgo Cluster

Virgo Cluster – Virgo

The bright star Spica lies at the bottom of the "y-shaped bowl" of Virgo, the maiden or virgin in Greek mythology. Inside the bowl is a cluster of galaxies called the "Virgo Cluster" containing some 1,300 galaxies [11]. This is the center of a larger object called the "Virgo Supercluster," of which the Local Group (and, therefore, the Milky Way) is a part. Incidentally, our cosmic address is:

Earth
Solar System
Milky Way Galaxy
Local Group
Virgo Supercluster
Universe

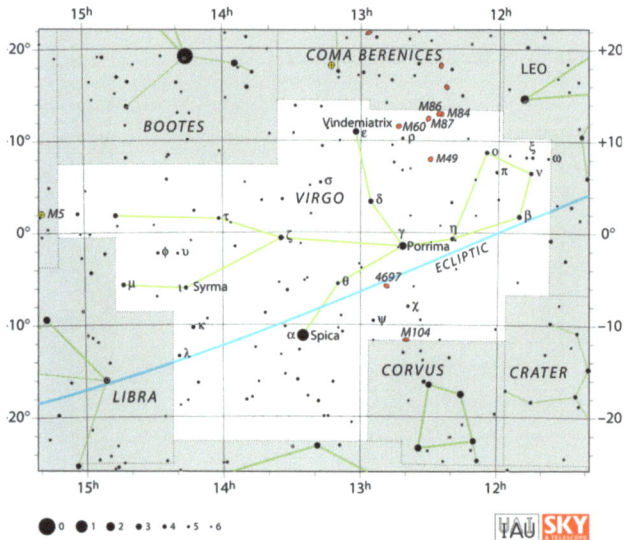

Fig. 19. Virgo Constellation

Fig. 20. Noondeshin Bemaadizid "Exhausted Bather"

NIIBIN ANANGOOG – SUMMER STARS

Noondeshin Bemaadizid –
Exhausted Bather – Hercules

The Exhausted Bather, *Noondeshin Bemaadizid,* is a person who has just completed a sweat lodge ceremony. The person is exhausted physically after participating in the sweat but full of life and renewed on the inside (spiritually). The Exhausted Bather is an early summer constellation. Note: At the head of the Bather is a fuzzy patch of white light. This is the globular cluster M13, which contains over 300,000 stars.

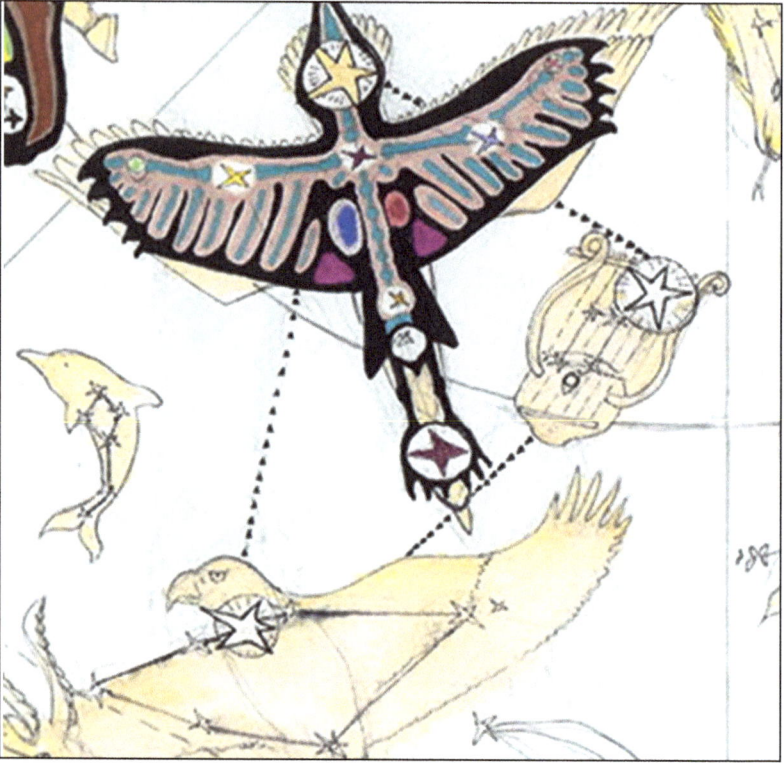

Fig. 21. Ajijaak (Crane)

Ajijaak – Crane / *Bineshi Okanin* – Skeleton Bird – Cygnus

The crane is one of the leaders in the Ojibwe clan system [12]. Cranes can grow almost as tall as a person with wingspans longer than most people's height. It is one of the tallest birds in the world and can fly very high. Crane and Loon lead the people to stay strong. This constellation is overhead a few hours after sunset in the summertime.

Fig. 22. Sandhill Crane

Nenabozho – Nenabozho – Scorpio

Nenabozho is a hero figure and a spirit that had many excursions on Earth a long time ago. He helped the people by creating dry land after the last flood. He had many human characteristics, such as making mistakes. There are many important *Nenabozho* stories that are traditionally told only when there is snow on the ground. Ojibwe storytellers are the keepers of the vast oral libraries of *Nenabozho* and other important cultural stories. This constellation shows *Nenabozho* shooting an arrow at the *Gaadidnaway* – Curly Tail/*Mishibizhii* – Great Panther. In June, a few hours after sunset, the *Nenabozho* constellation can be seen rising over the southeastern horizon shooting his arrow at *Gaadidnaway* – Curly Tail found setting in the West.

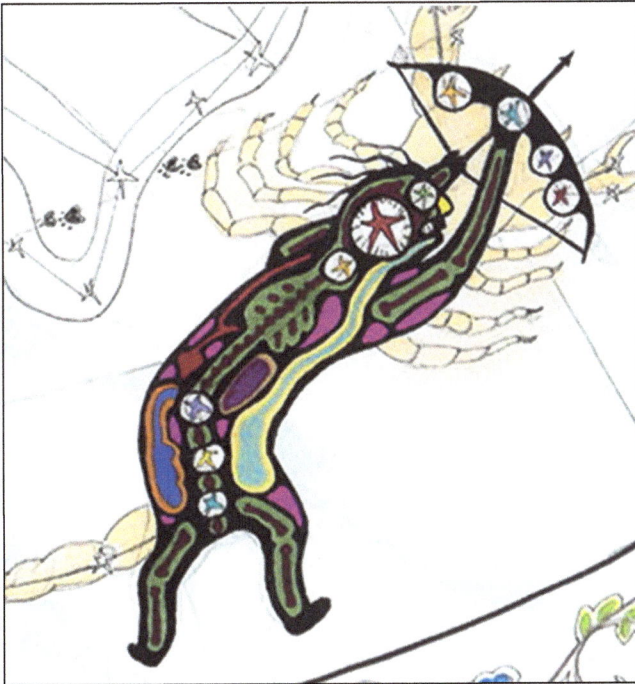

Fig. 23. Nanaboujou

Astronomical Treasures in the *Niibin Giizhig* – Summer Sky

Kepler Space Telescope

The Keplar Space telescope was launched in 2009 with the mission of determining how many other Earth-like (habitable) planets exist in our galaxy. It carefully observed over 145,000 stars while looking for a periodic dimming of starlight of roughly one part in 10,000. In an area the size of a fist held at arm's length (10°x10°), between the Greek constellations Cygnus and Lyra, the Kepler telescope found 961 confirmed exoplanets and very possibly another 3,000 (as of February 2014). Using this data, it is now estimated that there are as many planets in our galaxy as there are stars— 100 - 400 billion planets [13]. It is also estimated there are forty billion Earth-sized planets orbiting in the habitable zone (the right conditions for liquid water) around their star in the Milky Way galaxy.

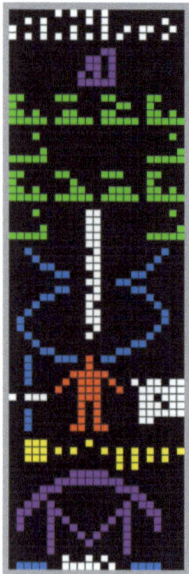

Fig. 24. Arecibo Message

Hercules – M13 and Arecibo Message

In 1974, a radio message was sent towards the globular star cluster M13 in Hercules. Using only two digits, 0 and 1, a three-minute binary code message about humans was broadcast. The message contained some of the following information: numbers, atomic numbers of elements that make up DNA, the world population at the time, human dimensions, the telescope dimensions, and the layout of the solar system. The star cluster M13 contains over 300,000 densely packed stars in the constellation Hercules. Traveling at the speed of light, roughly 186,000 miles per second, it will take 25,000 years for the message to arrive at M13.

Cygnus X-1

Also known as the Northern Cross, Cygnus the Swan contains one of the first-discovered stellar mass black holes. In 1964, astronomers found a strong x-ray source with no visible light counterpart coming from this position in the sky. Later research confirmed that Cygnus X-1 is part of an x-ray binary system. A large blue star, HDE 226868, is in a tight orbit with

Cygnus X-1. The blue star is losing material to the black hole. As this stolen gas and dust hits the accretion disk of Cygnus X-1, it is heated to millions of degrees and shines in high energy x-rays.

Fig. 25. Black Hole (simulated view)

M57, Ring Nebula

In the Ring Nebula, in the constellation Lyra the Harp in Greek mythology, is the last remnants of a dying star.

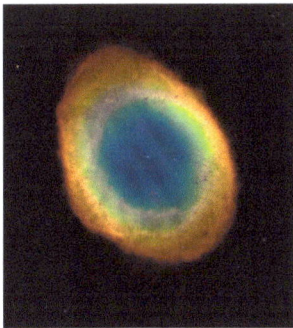

Unlike massive stars that end their lives more dramatically, this middle mass star, after having exhausted all of its hydrogen fuel, expels its outer layers over tens of thousands of years, like a snake shedding its skin. The hot core of the star emits ultraviolet light, which ionizes the surrounding gas until it glows. The heavier elements, made only by stars, are recycled into space for the next generation of stars ("nucleosynthesis"). At the center of every planetary nebula is the compact core of a once

Fig. 26. Ring Nebula M57

healthy star. This object is called a "white dwarf"; with only electron pressure holding up against gravity, it is estimated that one teaspoon of white dwarf material weighs approximately ten tons [14].

Center of MWG, Supermassive Black Hole

Within the Greek constellation Sagittarius the Teapot is the direction to the center of the Milky Way Galaxy. Approximately 26,000 light years away, there is a supermassive black hole at the very center of the galaxy. Known as Sgr A*, it has a mass of roughly four million suns. This was calculated using Kepler/Newton's laws (derived in the 1600s) and watching the very fast orbits of nearby stars around the supermassive black hole. The orbital speeds of these very close stars tell us the mass of the central object.

*Fig. 27. Sgr A**

DAGWAAGIN ANANGOOG – FALL STARS

Mooz – Moose – Pegasus, Lacerta

Like *Maang* – Loon and *Ajijaak* – Crane, the *Mooz* constellation represents an animal of the Ojibwe clan system. Moose provide food, clothing, and shelter for the people, much like deer or caribou. Compared to a deer, a moose is much bigger and spends a lot of time in the water, especially in summer. Male moose have a "beard" of skin under their chin that can be seen in the constellation. Traditionally, when a moose was killed for food, the beard was hung high on a tree branch to reflect the *Mooz* constellation because it literally could not be hung in the sky; it would be disrespectful for the moose's beard to be on the ground. This was a way to honor and thank the moose for giving its life.

Fig. 28. Mooz

Fig. 29. Pleiades

Bagone'giizhig –
Hole in the Sky – Pleiades/Seven Sisters

The hole in the sky refers to the Ojibwe shaking tent ceremony. The tent that the medicine person builds acts as a spiritual doorway that relates to the Pleiades/Seven Sisters star cluster. Seven poles were traditionally used to make the shaking tent. Each of the seven poles connects spiritually to one of the stars of *Bagone'giizhig* – Hole in the Sky – Pleiades/Seven Sisters. The top is intentionally left open to facilitate this connection. When the reflection happens, a doorway is opened, and spiritual connections are made. Note: Another version of the shaking tent uses thirteen different kinds of wooden posts. This signifies the thirteen moons in a year, the Ojibwe calendar. There are four different kinds of shaking tent.

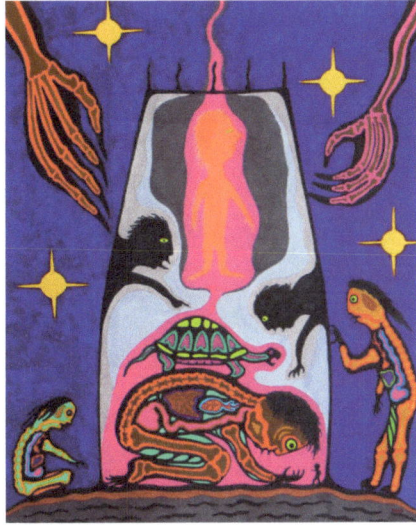

Fig. 30. Jiisakaan
(Shaking Tent)

Madoodoowasiniig – Sweating Stones – Pleiades/Seven Sisters

In the sweat lodge purification ceremony, basaltic rocks are heated in a central fire and brought into the center of the lodge. As the rocks glow a bright red-orange, they are returning to their original form, molten lava. The participants of the sweat lodge attempt to mirror this same behavior. Human beings come from the stars/spirit world, and the sweat lodge ceremony is about returning to a spiritual focus. Pleiades/Seven Sisters is seen overhead in late fall.

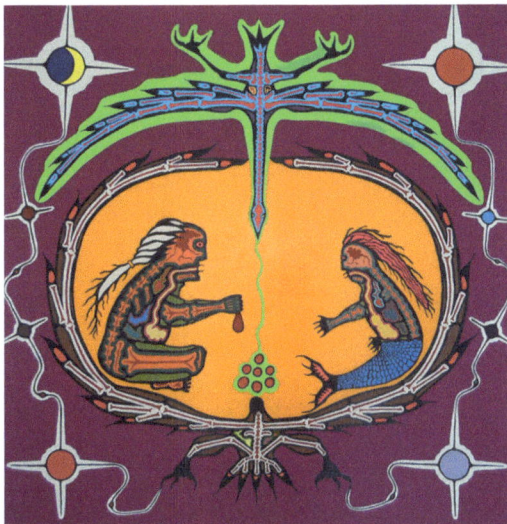

*Fig. 31.
Biindaakoojige
(Offering of
Tobacco)*

23

Astronomical Treasures in the *Dagwaagin Giizhig* – Fall Sky

Fig. 32. Andromeda Galaxy M31

M31, Andromeda Galaxy

At a distance of 2.5 million light years (one light year is approximately 6 trillion miles), the Andromeda Galaxy is the farthest object that can be seen with the naked eye. A spiral galaxy containing about twice the number of stars as the Milky Way Galaxy (roughly one trillion stars) [15], it is the largest member of the Local Group. Gravity is pulling the two galaxies together, and we are on a collision course with our "sister spiral" that is estimated to happen in approximately four billion years. Individual stars are unlikely to collide, but the gas and dust will interact gravitationally causing both galaxies to merge, lose their spiral shape, and become one large elliptical galaxy.

Fig. 33. The Mice Galaxies NGC 4676

Pleiades/Seven Sisters

Fig. 34. Pleiades

Pleiades is a young (100 million years old) cluster of stars seen in the Greek constellation Taurus the Bull. Its most massive stars shine brightly in hot blue light, which is scattered efficiently by the surrounding dust in the area and causes the entire nebula to glow in blue light (called a "reflection nebula"). This cluster of about 1,000 stars will eventually disperse. Many indigenous cultures have star knowledge relating to the Pleiades star cluster. It is known as Seven Sisters (Greek mythology), as *Subaru* ("Unite") in Japan [16] and as *Dilyehe* ("Pinlike Sparkles") in Dine/Navajo [17].

Fomalhaut b

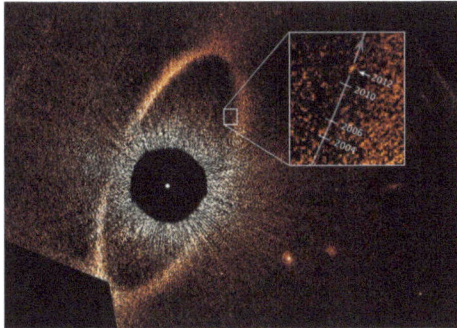

Fig. 35. Folmalhaut b

In 2008, using the Hubble Space Telescope, human beings photographed a direct image of another planet outside of our solar system for the first time. This planet orbits the star, Folmalhaut b, in the constellation Southern Pisces (Piscis Austrinus) about twenty-five light years away. The star system is very young, as indicated by the dusty accretion disk still in place around the central star. Fomalhaut b has an extremely wide orbit of 175 times the Earth-Sun distance and takes 2,000 years to complete one revolution.

BIBOON ANANGOOG – WINTER STARS

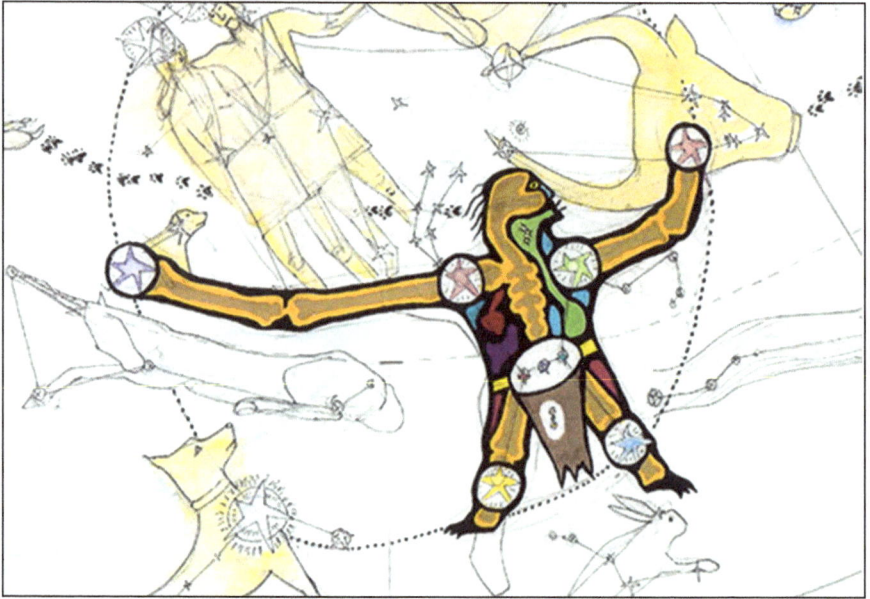

Fig. 36. Biboonikeonini (Wintermaker)

Biboonikeonini – Wintermaker –
Orion, Canis Minor, Aldebaran

Biboonikeonini – Wintermaker is a spirit that makes winter. Each season has
certain spirits that make the season happen. Winter-only stories are told in
wintertime because a person knows the winter spirits are there. No winter

*Fig. 37. North Lake
Hegman Pictographs*

stories are told after the frogs wake up. *Biboonikeonini* – Wintermaker is seen
in the North Hegman Lake pictographs. The rock painting shows the shape
of a strong Ojibwe canoe man [18]. His outstretched arms rule the winter
sky. The main body of *Biboonikeonini* – Wintermaker overlaps with the
Greek constellation Orion, but the left arm stretches to Canis Minor and
the right arm to Taurus. Altogether, *Biboonikeonini* – Wintermaker is about
four times the angular diameter of Orion. Wintermaker is seen
South/overhead during the winter months a few hours after sunset. Note:
In Ojibwe, the snow is referred to as "grandfathers"; for example,
"nimishoomis bangishin" is said when snow is falling and translates as
"grandfathers falling." The word "grandfathers" signifies the spirit part of
the snow, our connection to snow as a relative, and the observation that
snow is much older than humans.

Fig. 38. Biboonikeonini (Wintermaker) Reflected in Us

Astronomical Treasures in the *Biboon Giizhig* – Winter Sky

Fig. 39. Orion Nebula M42

M42, The Orion Nebula

In the area below the belt of Orion is a fuzzy patch of sky that is visible on a dark clear night with the naked eye. This is the Great Orion Nebula. Over 1,000 light years away, this huge area of star formation is twenty-four light years across. Using the Hubble Space Telescope, we have zoomed in to see newly forming stars complete with their proplanetary discs. For the first time in human history, we have taken images of distant "solar systems" forming. One of the things that the Orion Nebula teaches us is that planetary systems appear to be common.

Crab SNR

In the Greek constellation Taurus the Bull is the leftover cloud of a massive star that ran out of fuel and exploded in the form of a type II supernova. The Chinese and others recorded this event in 1054 AD. These violent explosions are the only known process in the universe to make most atoms. We are made of star stuff [19]. Western scientists call this process "nucleosynthesis." The same idea is taught in the Ojibwe culture. When a person dies, it is said *"shiikawasegaa,"* which means "no more light, the light moves on" and refers to the spirit as starlight.

Fig. 40. Crab Pulsar M1

What remains of the original star after the supernova explosion is one of the most compact objects known, a neutron star. The incredible pull of gravity is balanced only by quantum mechanical pressure from the neutrons. One teaspoon of neutron star weighs about 100 million tons [20]. This particular neutron star is spinning about thirty times around in one second. Its poles are directly towards our line of sight, and we receive a radio pulse from it every thirty-three milliseconds. The pulsar star is about the size of a small city (twelve miles in diameter).

Fig. 41. Biboonikeonini (Wintermaker)

Betelgeuse, a Cool, Dying, Giant Star

At the top left shoulder of *Biboonikeonini* – Wintermaker, or the Orion constellation in Greek mythology, is Betelgeuse, a star in its last moments of life. As it struggles to find balance after running out of its main fuel, hydrogen, the outer layers swell up, and the star cools in temperature. Betelgeuse is a reddish color star. If we replaced Betelguese with the Sun, its outer layers would extend past the orbit of Mars. The Earth would be inside the swollen, dying star. Our Sun is expected to become a red giant in about 4.5 billion years. Within *Biboonikeonini* – Wintermaker, compare this red, cool star with the bottom right bluish star, Rigel. Rigel is also a dying star, but nuclear processes have allowed it to maintain a very high temperature, about twice the temperature of the Sun (about 20,000° F) [21].

IKWE ANANG – VENUS

Venus is the third brightest object in the sky after the Sun and the Moon. It is so bright that it is often mistaken for a UFO because Venus is the closest planet to us at roughly twenty-five million miles (compared to Mars at forty-seven million miles at closest approach). Its brightness is due to light reflected from the Sun; like Earth and all terrestrial planets, Venus does not generate any visible light. Venus' light is especially bright because it is covered in white, reflective clouds. For this reason, people in the early twentieth century had a fascination with "life on Venus" because we could not see what was underneath the sulfuric acid clouds. In the 1960s, the first missions used radar wavelengths to cut through the cloud layer and see the topography underneath. We found extensive volcanism [22]. At one time, Venus could have had oceans, but due to the runaway greenhouse effect, Venus is now the hottest planet in the Solar System (~800 °F). The heat, combined with the shut down of Venus' magnetic field, would have caused the water molecules to separate into hydrogen and oxygen ("photo-dissociation") and the hydrogen atoms to be stripped away by the solar wind [23]. Despite its desert-like volcanic surface, Venus is closest to Earth in size, density, and gravity and is nicknamed Earth's "Sister planet."

Fig. 42. Venus: visible wavelengths (left), radar (right)

Ojibwe Connection to Venus

In Ojibwe star knowledge, Venus is known as *Ikwe Anang* – Women's Star (C. Gawboy, unpublished data). The name has multiple layers of meaning. The first understanding is that native Ojibwe people carefully observed the motion of Venus each day/night and found patterns in the movement. The pattern of Venus' movement as seen from an observer on Earth is that Venus will appear in the East before sunrise (the Morning Star) and then in the West just after sunset (the Evening Star). The pattern repeats on a nine-month cycle. As a person watches Venus in the morning for about nine months, it disappears for a short time and then reappears in the opposite sky at sunset for about nine months. Then, the cycle repeats (see Appendix for Cycles of Venus). Remarkably, this nine-month cycle is the same timespan as human gestation. This is why Ojibwe and other indigenous cultures have associated Venus with the feminine.

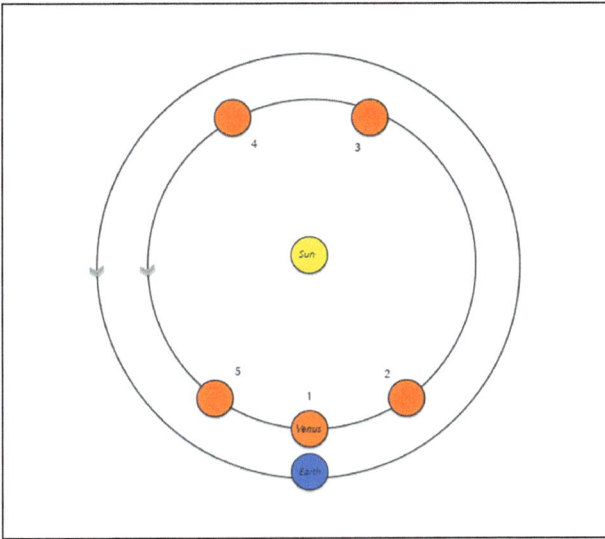

Fig. 43. Venus-Earth orbit around the Sun, multiple views of Venus in orbit

Another connection between Venus and women is that traditional Ojibwe women were responsible for gathering the water and would awaken before sunrise to do so [24]. Venus is also called *Waaban Anang* – East Star (Morning Star) because it is visible for about half of its cycle in the East just before sunrise.

Fig. 44. Listening to Ikwe Anang (Women's Star)

MOON

Traditionally, the Ojibwe people used the Sun, Moon, and stars to keep track of the passing of time. Like many indigenous cultures, a lunar calendar was used that related to important seasonal events. The word "month" is derived from *moneth,* which comes from "moon" [25]. On average, the Moon takes 29.5 day to make one circle around the Earth as seen from our backyard. Twelve moon months have too few days for a year (354 days), and thirteen moon months have too many days for a year (383.5 days) as compared to the 365 days in a solar year. For this reason, only certain years have thirteen moons.

In the Ojibwe language, the name of the Moon each month signifies whatever is happening that is important to survival at that time, such as the gathering of food. For example, June is *Ode'imini-giizis* – Strawberry Moon, the time of year that the strawberries are ripe. It is the only time of year when it happens; if you miss out, you have to wait until next year to gather

Fig. 45. Gekinoo'amaaged (Teacher)

strawberries or hope to trade with someone for berries.

Ojibwe time keeping also differs from Western time keeping because the name of the Moon changes with location, especially latitude. For example, the *Onaabani-giizis* – Maple Sap Boiling Moon is in April at Fond du Lac near Cloquet, Minnesota (50° N), but in Thunder Bay, Ontario, Canada there are no maple trees, so this Moon is *Biigaadayan-giizis* "When Lakes are Open." *Waatebagaa-giizis* – Leaves Changing Color Moon indicates September at Fond du Lac, but in Canada, the leaves change earlier, so *Waatebagaa-giizis* indicates August.

Traditional Ojibwe people also kept track of time using the phases of the Moon and the lunar calendar. For example, in reference to his or her birthday, a person would say, "I was born on the full moon during the *Manoominike-giizis* – Ricing Moon."

Throughout many indigenous cultures, the Moon has a close connection to the feminine and fertility. This is due to the menstruation cycle of women being approximately the same length as one cycle of the Moon (29.5 days). In Ojibwe, the Moon is called *"Dibik-giizis"* ("Night Sun") and also "Grandmother Moon."

CONCLUSION

The work presented here is interdisciplinary: astronomy, culture, art, and language are each represented. The delivery of an in-depth, interdisciplinary topic like indigenous astronomy can be overwhelming to students, adults, or youth who have grown up with light pollution, tall buildings, and computers. Unlike traditional native people, we today tend to spend a lot of time indoors. Most people, however, have at least some familiarity with the Big Dipper, Sun, and Moon. The delivery of this culturally rich material must be simple, yet allow for complexity and abstraction. To achieve this goal, we first use the cultural framework of the four directions. The current night sky is subdivided into North, East, South/overhead, and West; thus, from the beginning of the discussion, the cultural context is intact. The four directions are considered an important framework and guideposts in native culture. This instructional approach builds on a sense of place [26] and allows participants to orientate the current night sky with the cardinal directions. The technique grounds the complexity of the current night sky in the tangible and the simple, yet creates a multi-layered, circular learning approach. Following this approach allows for the widest range of participants to take part in the learning experience.

Furthermore, the stars and constellations can be best understood in terms of the four seasons. The discussion is simplified again by fixing the time as a few hours after sunset. This is the observing time and is referred to as "prime time" for stargazing. Only in the northern direction will the circumpolar stars, or northern stars as seen from approximately 45-55° N latitude/85-110° W longitude, be visible throughout the year. When an observer faces due South (azimuth 180° along the horizon), he/she will see the current season of stars. The previous season will be seen setting in the West and the following season will be seen rising in the East. The *Ojibwe Giizhig Anang Masinaa'igan* – Ojibwe Sky Star Map is best presented by transforming the discussion into an experiential, hands-on event. In addition, this highly visual, holistic, and cooperative learning environment is consistent with a traditional native learning style [27].

Finally, we encourage mindfulness of cultural protocols. Native knowledge is sometimes a different way of knowing than Western science. There are strict cultural protocols that must be respected, such as when some stories

Fig. 47. The Stars Are Looking Back at Us

are to be told. For example, some are only told when there is snow on the ground. We must be extremely careful not to introduce or propagate error into the written or oral records. Use caution and be hesitant. Users of these materials are urged to seek out elders and native community members to bring into the classroom. Materials represented here should be viewed as a beginning. *Miigwech. Pidamaya/Pilamaya.* Thank you.

"Everything you need is in the Stars…" [28]

Fig. 46. Everything You Need Is in the Stars

APPENDIX

Ojibwe Months/Moons (Fond du Lac region) [29]

Month	*Ojibwe*	English
January	*Gichimanidoo-giizis*	Great Spirit Moon
February	*Namebini-giizis*	Sucker Fish Moon
March	*Onaabani-giizis*	Hard Crust on the Snow Moon
April	*Iskigamizige-giizis*	Maple Sap Boiling Moon
May	*Zaagibagaa-giizis*	Budding Moon
June	*Ode'imini-giizis*	Strawberry Moon
July	*Aabita-niibino-giizis*	Mid-summer Moon
August	*Manoominike-giizis*	Ricing Moon
September	*Waatebagaa-giizis*	Leaves Changing Color Moon
October	*Binaakwii-giizis*	Falling Leaves Moon
November	*Gashkadino-giizis*	Freezing Moon
December	*Manidoo-giizisoons*	Little Spirit Moon

Ojibwe Celestial Vocabulary

English	*Ojibwe*
Star	*Anang (Anung)*
Star World	*Anang aki*
Moon	*Dibik-giizis (Night Sun)*
Sun	*Giizis*
Sky	*Giizhig*
Venus	*Ikwe Anang (Women's Star)*
Venus - Evening Star	*Onaagoshi Anang*
Venus - Morning Star	*Waaban Anang*
Ecliptic	*Ma'iingan Mikan (Wolf Trail)*
Milky Way (MW)	*Jiibaykona (Spirit Path)*
Milky Way (MW)	*Jiibay Ziibi (River of Souls)*
Meteor/Falling star	*Bangishin Anang*
Universe	*Gaagige Giizhig (Forever Sky), Ishpeming (the Sky Above)*
Aurora Borealis (Northern Lights)	*Jiibayag niimi'idiwa (the Spirits are dancing)*
Aurora Borealis (Northern Lights)	*Waawaate*
Star Knowledge (Wisdom)	*Anang Nibwakawin*
(Sky) Star map	*Giizhig Anang Masinaa'igan*
EAST	*Waaban*
WEST	*Ningaabii'an*
NORTH	*Giiwedin*
SOUTH	*Zhaawan*

Ojibwe Celestial Vocabulary

	Ojibwe	**Related Greek Constellations**
ZIIGWAN - SPRING		
Curly Tail, Great Panther	*Gaadidnaway, Mishibizhii*	Leo, Hydra
Sweat Lodge	*Madoodiswan*	Corona
BIBOON - WINTER		
Wintermaker	*Biboonikeonini*	Orion, Canis Minor, Taurus
GIIWEDIN - NORTH		
Loon	*Maang*	Little Dipper
Fisher	*Ojiig*	Big Dipper
North Star	*Giiwedin Anang*	Polaris
DAGWAAGIN - FALL		
Moose	*Mooz*	Pegasus, Lacerta
Hole in the Sky	*Bagone'giizhig*	Pleiades
Sweating Stones	*Madoodoowasiniig*	Pleiades
NIIBIN - SUMMER		
Crane/Skeleton Bird	*Ajijaak/Bineshi Okanin*	Cygnus
Exhausted Bather/Person	*Noondeshin Bemaadizid*	Hercules
Nenabozho	*Nenabozho*	Scorpio

Cycles of Venus

Position	Phase of Venus	Other comments/names associated with this position
1	New	Not visible, also called "Inferior Conjunction"
1-2	Waxing Crescent	Not visible
2	Waxing Crescent	Venus first visible in the East before Sunrise, called the "Morning Star"
2-3	Moving from Waxing Crescent through First Quarter to Waxing Gibbous	Venus is seen as the Morning Star for about 9 months.
3	Waxing Gibbous	The last day that Venus is visible as the Morning Star
3-4	Moving from Waxing Gibbous to Full (directly in line with the Earth-Sun) to Waning Gibbous	Not visible
4	Waning Gibbous	Venus first visible in the West at Sunset, called the "Evening Star"
4-5	Moving from Waning Gibbous through Last Quarter to Waning Crescent	Venus is seen as the Evening Star for about 9 months.
5	Waning Crescent	The last day that Venus is visible as the Evening Star
5-1	Moving from Waning Crescent to New, the cycle repeats.	Not visible

FIGURES

Fig. 1. *Ojibwe Giizhig Anung Masinaa'igan (Ojibwe Sky Star Map)*. Painted by Annette S. Lee & William Wilson. Language by William Wilson. Watercolor & mixed media on paper, 36 x 36," 2012.

Fig. 2. Pictographs at North Hegman Lake, Boundary Waters Canoe Area, Minnesota. Photo by Annette S. Lee, 2011.

Fig. 3. *Ojiig* (Fisher). William Wilson. Acrylic on canvas, 24 x 24," 2014.

Fig. 4. Ojiig (Fisher). Close up, *Ojibwe Giizhig Anung Masinaa'igan (Ojibwe Sky Star Map)*. Painted by Annette S. Lee & William Wilson. Language by William Wilson. Watercolor & mixed media on paper, 36 x 36," 2012.

Fig. 5. Maang. Close up, *Ojibwe Giizhig Anung Masinaaigan (Ojibwe Sky Star Map)*. Painted by Annette S. Lee & William Wilson. Language by William Wilson. Watercolor & mixed media on paper, 36 x 36," 2012.

Fig. 6. *Ishpiming Maang (Loon in the Sky)*. William Wilson. Acrylic on canvas, 36 x 36," 2012.

Fig. 7. *Maang (Loon) - Doorkeeper of the North*. Annette S. Lee. Mixed media painting on panel, 18 x 24," 2014.

Fig. 8. Hubble Deep Field Observing Geometry, NASA image public domain, 2007.

Fig. 9. Hubble Deep Field (full mosaic), NASA image public domain, 1996.

Fig. 10. Cepheus Constellation Map, IAU and *Sky & Telescope Magazine* (Roger Sinnott & Rick Fienberg), 2011.

Fig. 11. Earth Precession, NASA, Vectorized by Mysid in Inkscape after a NASA Earth Observatory image in Milutin Milankovitch Precession.

Fig. 12. Pictographs at North Hegman Lake. Boundary Waters Canoe Area, Minnesota. Photo by Annette S. Lee, 2011.

Fig. 13. Gaadidnaway (Curly Tail). Close up, *Ojibwe Giizhig Anung Masinaa'igan (Ojibwe Sky Star Map)*. Painted by Annette S. Lee & William Wilson. Language by William Wilson. Watercolor & mixed media on paper, 36 x 36," 2012.

Fig. 14. Madoodiswan (Sweat Lodge). Close up, *Ojibwe Giizhig Anung Masinaa'igan (Ojibwe Sky Star Map)*. Painted by Annette S. Lee & William Wilson. Language by William Wilson. Watercolor & Mixed Media on paper, 36 x 36," 2012.

Fig. 15. *Iskigamizigan (Sugar Bush Camp)*. William Wilson. Art marker on paper, 11 x 17," 2007.

Fig. 16. *Nookomiss Kikinoamgewin (Grandmother Teaching)*. Annette S. Lee. Acrylic on canvas, 25 x 31," 2012.

Fig. 17. *Zaabibagaa and Spring Stars*. Annette S. Lee. Watercolor on paper, 8 x 17," 2011.

Fig. 18. Virgo Cluster, Chris Mihos (Case Western Reserve University)/ESO, 2009.

Fig. 19. Virgo Constellation, IAU and *Sky & Telescope Magazine* (Roger Sinnott & Rick Fienberg), 2011.

Fig. 20. Bather. Close up, *Ojibwe Giizhig Anung Masinaa'igan (Ojibwe Sky Star Map)*. Painted by Annette S. Lee & William Wilson. Language by William Wilson. Watercolor & mixed media on paper, 36 x 36," 2012.

Fig. 21. Ajijaak (Crane). Close up, *Ojibwe Giizhig Anung Masinaa'igan (Ojibwe Sky Star Map)*. Painted by Annette S. Lee & William Wilson. Language by William Wilson. Watercolor & mixed media on paper, 36 x 36," 2012.

Fig. 22. Sandhill crane flying near Gibbon, Nebraska. Photo by A. M. Fellegy, 2014.

Fig. 23. Nanaboujou. Close up, *Ojibwe Giizhig Anung Masinaa'igan (Ojibwe Sky Star Map)*. Painted by Annette S. Lee & William Wilson. Language by William Wilson. Watercolor & mixed media on paper, 36 x 36," 2012.

Fig. 24. Arecibo message as sent 1974 from the Arecibo Observatory, Arne Nordmann, 2005.

Fig. 25. *Black Hole*. Simulated view of a black hole in front of the Large Magellanic Cloud, Alain r, 2006.

Fig. 26. *Ring Nebula M57*. Hubble Heritage Team (AURA/STScI/NASA), 1998.

Fig. 27. *Sgr A**. Chandra (x-ray) image based on data from one million seconds or almost two weeks, NASA/CXC/MIT/F. Baganoff, R. Shcherbakov et al., 2010.

Fig. 28. Mooz. Close up, *Ojibwe Giizhig Anung Masinaa'igan (Ojibwe Sky Star Map)*. Painted by Annette S. Lee & William Wilson. Language by William Wilson. Watercolor & mixed media on paper, 36 x 36," 2012.

Fig. 29. Pleiades. Close up, *Ojibwe Giizhig Anung Masinaa'igan (Ojibwe Sky Star Map)*. Painted by Annette S. Lee & William Wilson. Language by William Wilson. Watercolor & mixed media on paper, 36 x 36," 2012.

Fig. 30. *Jiisakaan (Shaking Tent)*. William Wilson. Art marker on paper, 11 x 17," 2008.

Fig. 31. *Biindaakoojige (Offering of Tobacco)*. William Wilson. Acrylic on canvas, 36 x 36," 2014.

Fig. 32. *Andromeda Galaxy M31*. Adam Evans, 2010.

Fig. 33. *The Mice Galaxies NGC 4676*. NASA, H. Ford (JHU), G. Illingworth (UCSC/LO), M.Clampin (STScI), G. Hartig (STScI), the ACS Science Team, and ESA, 2002.

Fig. 34. *Pleiades M45*. NASA, ESA, AURA/Caltech, Palomar Observatory, 2004.

Fig. 35. *Fomalhaut b*. NASA and ESA, 2013.

Fig. 36. Biboonkeonini (Wintermaker). Close up, *Ojibwe Giizhig Anung Masinaa'igan (Ojibwe Sky Star Map)*. Painted by Annette S. Lee & William Wilson. Language by William Wilson. Watercolor & mixed media on paper, 36 x 36," 2012.

Fig. 37. Pictographs at North Hegman Lake, Boundary Waters Canoe Area, Minnesota. Photo by Annette S. Lee, 2011.

END NOTES

1. Morton, R. and Gawboy, C. 2003. *Talking Rocks: Geology and 10,000 Years of Native American Tradition in the Lake Superior Region.* Minneapolis: University of Minnesota Press.

2. Goodman, R. 1992. *Lakota Star Knowledge: Studies in Lakota Stellar Theology.* Mission SD: Sinte Gleska University.

3. P. Schultz, personal communication.

4. Minnesota Department of Education. 2010, "Minnesota Academic Standards – Science K-12." <http://education.state.mn.us/MDE/EdExc/StanCurri/K-12Academic Standards/index.htm>

5. C. Gawboy, unpublished data

6. See Note 1.

7. See Note 1.

8. See Note 1.

9. Benton-Banai, E. 2010. *The Mishomis Book: The Voice of the Ojibway.* Hayward: Indian Country Communications, Inc., Minneapolis: University of Minnesota Press.

10. <http://en.wikipedia.org/wiki/Loon>

11. <http://en.wikipedia.org/wiki/Virgo_cluster>

12. See Note 9.

13. <http://en.wikipedia.org/wiki/Kepler_(spacecraft)>

14. Seeds, M. 2008. *Stars and Galaxies.* Belmont, CA: Brooks/Cole.

15. <http://en.wikipedia.org/wiki/Milky_Way_Galaxy>

16. Krupp, E. 1992. *Beyond the Blue Horizon: Myths and Legends of the Sun, Moon, Stars and Planets.* New York: Oxford University Press.

17. Maryboy, N. and Begay, D. 2010. *Sharing the Skies: Navajo Astronomy.* Tucson: Rio Nuevo Publishers.

18. See Note 1.

19. Sagan, C. 1980. *Cosmos.* New York: Random House

20. See Note 14.

21. <http://en.wikipedia.org/wiki/Betelgeuse>

22. Head, J., L. S. Crumpler, J. Aubele, J. Guest, and R. Saunders. 1992. "Venus Volcanism: Classification of Volcanic Features and Structures, Associations, and Global Distribution from Magellan Data." *Journal of Geophysical Research: Planets (1991–2012)* 97, no. E8: 13153-13197.

23. "Caught in the wind from the Sun." ESA (Venus Express). 28 November 2007. Retrieved 2008-07-12.

24. C. Gawboy, personal communication.

25. <http://wiki.answers.com/Q/The_original_meaning_of_the_word_month>

26. Semken, S. 2005. "Sense of Place and Place-Based Introductory Geoscience Teaching for American Indian and Alaska Native Undergraduates." *Journal of Geoscience Education* 53, 149-157.

27. Cleary, L. Miller and Peacock, T. 1997. *Collected Wisdom: American Indian Education.* Boston: Allyn and Bacon.

28. Anonymous Ojibwe elders.

29. Ojibwe Language Society. 1998.

www.ingramcontent.com/pod-product-compliance
Lightning Source LLC
Chambersburg PA
CBHW040930030426

42334CB00002B/24